CCSS **Genre** Fantasy

MW00484326

Essential Question
What is it like where you live?

by Erin Matthews
illustrated by Roberta Collier Morales

It's harvest time on the farm!
Everyone is helping.

"I like harvest time," says Pig.
"Everything is ripe and ready
to pick."

"I'll pick the corn," says Pig.

"I'll pick the pumpkins,"
says Goose.

"I'll pick the apples," says Dog.

Chapter 2

Everyone Helps

Pig looks out at the corn.

"This is nice corn," he says.

"It is very nice, Pig," says Goose.
"It will sell well at the market."

Goose looks down at the pumpkins.

"These are nice pumpkins," she says.

"They are very nice, Goose," says Dog. "They will sell well at the market."

Dog looks up at the apples.

"These are nice apples," he says.

"They are very nice, Dog,"
says Pig. "They will sell well at
the market."

6

Chapter 3

Off to Market!

"We are finished," says Pig.

"Let's load the cart," says Goose.

Pig, Goose, and Dog fill the cart with apples, pumpkins, and corn.

"We are ready to go to market!" says Dog.

Pig, Goose, and Dog hop on the cart. They drive down to the river.

"Oh, no! The bridge is down," says Pig.

"We can't get the harvest to market," says Goose.

"What will we do?" asks Dog.

Chapter 4

Clever Beaver

"I know someone who can help us," says Pig.

"Who is it?" asks Goose.

"Beaver can help us!" says Dog.

Pig, Goose, and Dog talk to
Beaver.

"The bridge is down," says Pig.

"We have to cross the river,"
says Goose.

"Can you help us?" asks Dog.

Beaver makes a new bridge.

"Beaver did it!" says Pig.

"Thank you, Beaver!" says Dog.

"Now we can get to market," says Goose. "We can sell our apples, pumpkins, and corn!"

Respond to Reading

Retell

Use your own words to retell details in *Harvest Time*.

Detail	Detail	Detail

Text Evidence

1. Look at page 8. What happens after the friends go down to the river? Key Details

2. What details tell you that Beaver fixed the bridge?

   Key Details

3. How do you know *Harvest Time* is a fantasy? Genre

Compare Texts
Read about where some children live.

Where We Live

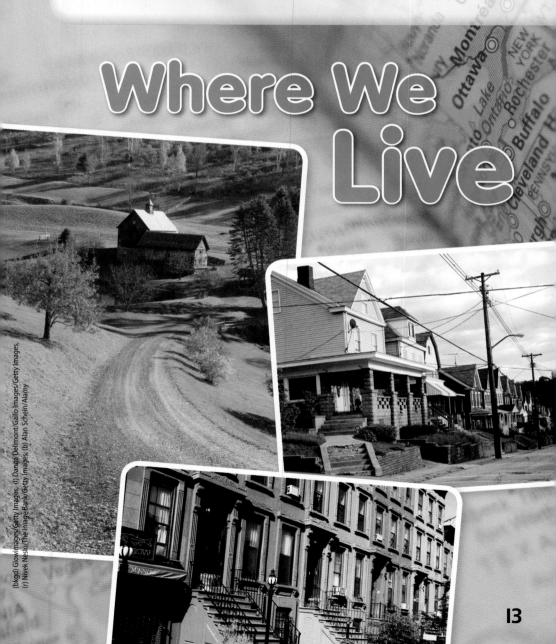

I live in the city.
My family lives
in an apartment.
We live on a
busy street.

Skate Park

My Home

Corner
Store

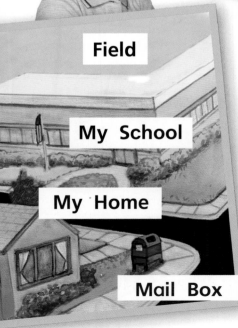

Field

My School

My Home

Mail Box

I live in a town.
There are lots of
trees and grass
on our street.
Mom walks me
to school.

Sell your books at sellbackyourBook.com!
Go to sellbackyourBook.com and get an instant price quote. We even pay the shipping - see what your old books are worth today!

Inspected By: maria_corral

00038533191

0003853 **3191** S

I live in the country.
We have cows and a pig.
There are fish in our pond.

My Home

Apple
Orchard

Pond

Make Connections
How are the places in the two stories
the same? How are they different?

Text to Text

Focus on
Social Studies

Purpose To explain what it is like where you live

What to Do

Step 1 ▶ Draw a picture of the place where you live. Remember to draw things you see outside.

Step 2 ▶ Write labels that explain what is special about where you live.

Step 3 ▶ Sit with a partner and share your pictures.
What things are the same?
What things are different?